WRESTLING

WRITTEN BY DOUG MARX

ROURKE CORPORATION, INC.
VERO BEACH, FLORIDA 32964

PRO-AM
SPORTS

The Rourke Corporation, Inc.
P.O. Box 3328, Vero Beach, FL 32964

Marx, Doug
    Wrestling/Doug Marx.
        p. cm.—(Pro-am sports)
    Includes index.
    ISBN 0-86593-347-2
    1. Wrestling—Juvenile literature. I. Title. II. Series.
    GV1195.M34 1993
    796.8'12—dc20   93-38544
                                                   CIP
                                                   AC

Cover photograph: Allsport (Mike Powell)
Interior Photographs:
Allsport 4, 15 bottom, 32 (Mike Powell); 10, 34 (Richard
    Martin/Agence Vandystadt); 22 (Gerard
    Vandystadt); 25 bottom, 27 (Shaun Botterill)
Denver Post 12, 15 top, 18, 20
Doug Marx 5, 26, 28, 30
Photo Researchers, Inc. 7 (Gerard Vandystadt)
UPI/Bettmann 11
USA Wrestling 8, 14, 17 (Doug Prediger/Lehigh
University), 23, 25 top, 29, 35 (U.S. Naval Academy)
Wide World Photos 36, 40, 42

Series Editor: Gregory Lee
Book design and production:
The Creative Spark, San Clemente, CA

Printed in the USA

The personal challenge of wrestling pits strength against strength in a one-on-one match.

CONTENTS

HOT TIP:
Want to know how to do a takedown?
Turn to page 24.

The moment of triumph, when the referee signals the victor in an Olympic wrestling match.

The Oldest Sport

CHAPTER ONE

Like bear cubs or puppies, a couple of young boys roll around on the grass, laughing, struggling with each other, trying to see who can hold the other down. They are not fighting. Their intention is not to hurt one another. They are testing one another's strength, quickness, and agility. Their rowdy, boisterous play is natural and all in fun. Writhing, squirming, wriggling out of each other's grasp, they are engaged in humanity's oldest, most universal sport: wrestling.

Wrestling is a weaponless combat sport. Today's contests take place indoors on a thick mat, inside a nine meter (almost 30 feet) diameter circle. Two males of equal weight face off in an intense struggle that can last up to six minutes requiring brains, balance, muscle, stamina, and lots of heart and desire. Unlike boxing or the martial arts, no punches or kicks are thrown. Wrestlers go at it hand-to-hand. Throwing an opponent off balance, or pinning him to the ground, is the essence of wrestling— the way to victory.

The cradle is one type of pin used in freestyle wrestling.

Modern wrestling is an amateur sport that has evolved from prehistoric times, when all the earth's inhabitants lived in tribes. Wrestling was often the way a tribe's leader was determined without demanding bloodshed and killing.

These early wrestling matches were sophisticated and filled with ritual and practice, not scratch-and-claw contests. A similar activity can be seen in the animal world when two stags lock horns, or when male baboons fight to see who will be the colony's new leader. Wrestling has also served as a kind of practice warfare. Even today there are Indian tribes in the Amazon basin of South America who wrestle every day, keeping themselves fit in case of intruders.

The sport of wrestling has nothing to do with politics and war, but everything to do with the individual athlete. It can give form and skill to a young male athlete's need to test himself hand-to-hand with a competitor of equal size. Unlike team sports, in which individuality is often sacrificed for the sake of the group, wrestling teaches self-reliance and provides an outlet for self-expression. It is a sport for athletes of all shapes and sizes. Because of the strength and balance required to wrestle well, together with the dozens of tricky moves that must be practiced and mastered, wrestling is a sport that calls for top conditioning of both mind and body. Like boxing, wrestling can be rough and bruising, and is still considered an all-male sport.

This book will present specific ways a young athlete can get involved in wrestling. Practice and conditioning will be discussed, along with some basic skills. The historical and international dimension of wrestling will also be investigated, as a good athlete should know about the traditions of his or her sport as well as its technical aspects.

Wrestling Around the World

References to wrestling matches appear in the earliest documents of ancient civilization. For example, there is a match described in *The Epic of Gilgamesh*, the oldest book in the world, written 4,000 years ago on clay tablets by a Sumerian poet. The ancient Greek poet, Homer, describes a wrestling contest in his book, *The Iliad*; and Greek mythology is filled with matches between gods such as Hercules and Antaeus. Jacob wrestling the Angel is a story from the Old Testament, a scene captured in a famous painting by Paul Gaugin. Similar age-old wrestling traditions exist in Egypt, India, China, and Japan. Among the Indians of North, Central, and South America, wrestling is a time-honored sport.

Although wrestling is universal, its styles are not. There are three basic styles of wrestling: the belt-and-jacket, the catch-hold, and the loose. All three are ancient.

Sumo wrestlers such as Maegashira compete in a form of belt wrestling requiring massive weight combined with surprising agility.

In belt-and-jacket wrestling, the clothing of the contestants becomes the principal way of getting a grip on one's opponent. A Japanese style called *judo* is an example of belt-and-jacket wrestling. The Japanese style called *sumo*—Japan's national sport—is an example of wrestling in which only a belt is worn. In sumo wrestling, huge 300-pound men attempt to bump and throw one another out of a circle. Belt-wrestling has been popular among many cultures since the dawn of human time. The ancient Mesopotamians practiced it, as do athletes today in Switzerland, Iceland, and Russia. The object in these matches is to throw or topple one's opponent so that some part of his body other than his feet touches the ground.

The catch-hold style requires the contestants to seize each other bodily with a certain grip before the match begins. Sometimes they must maintain this grip throughout the struggle. Catch-hold wrestling has been popular in such northern countries as England and Scotland. An Irish catch-hold style known as

Two Olympic wrestlers in a hand and collar tie-up resemble the scufflers of the nineteenth century.

"scuffling," in which the wrestlers grip each other "collar-and-elbow" (around the collarbone and elbow) became popular during the American Civil War. Abraham Lincoln was said to be a scuffler capable of holding his own. Indeed, baseball might be our national sport, but wrestling is our national heartbeat. In some parts of the United States, such as the Midwest, wrestling is as popular as basketball and football.

Changing Styles

Loose style wrestling is closest to the style seen today. Basically, loose wrestling is an open form in which the wrestlers begin the match separated and are free to use any grip they choose—except one that grabs hold of clothing. Evidence of the practice of loose wrestling has been found in ancient India, China, and Japan. North American Indians engaged in loose wrestling long before Columbus discovered the New World, and the explorer James Cook saw South Sea Islanders practice the sport. In most loose style wrestling, the winner is determined by a *touch fall* or a pin fall, otherwise known as a *pin*. In the touch fall, an opponent must be forced to lie supine—on his back—for a brief instant. The pin requires that an opponent be held in that position for a measurable length of time—usually two seconds. No further grappling occurs on the ground.

Loose wrestling was the favorite style of the ancient Greeks. During the nineteenth century, the French developed a style of loose wrestling called Greco-Roman, in honor of the Olympic tradition. In Greco-Roman wrestling, no holds are permitted below the waist, and the use of the legs in the contest for tripping your opponent is forbidden. This was the main style of wrestling in Europe until the late nineteenth century, when the more exciting and fast-paced catch-as-catch-can style was invented in the United States. As its name implies, catch-as-catch-can wrestling allows all forms of grips and holds—including head-locks and leg scissorholds. As catch-as-catch-can became popular, it was refined by the Amateur Athletic Union (AAU) and evolved into today's favorite, international freestyle wrestling. This form is a combination of the Greco-Roman and catch-as-catch-can styles.

Freestyle wrestling is the style most often used in American competition today. Because a fall or pin is not always achieved in a match, freestyle uses a point system based on each wrestler's control over his opponent, and the escapes, reversals, and near-pins he achieves. In the United States, from public schools to universities, more than one million wrestlers keep the sport alive, finding out what they are made of in the process.

Greco-Roman wrestling is the style used in the Olympic Games. International freestyle wrestling combines elements from Greco-Roman with other styles.

Wrestling's First Hero

Way back in the 1890s, rough-and-tumble wrestlers would barnstorm around the country. Going from town to town, they challenged one and all. These men wrestled for money, and their catch-as-catch-can style included "choke" and "submission" holds that could render an opponent unconscious. Sometimes their matches went on for hours, with short rest spells between lengthy periods being a real necessity. They were the first professional wrestlers.

The greatest grappler of this no-holds-barred era was Frank Gotch, who grew up in Iowa. In 1901, still a teenager, he "lit out" for the Alaska gold rush. Moving from camp to camp, he wrestled local talent for big money. He never lost. Seldom pinning his man, he preferred to make him say "uncle." In six months, Gotch returned home with $30,000 in his pocket! He was soon on tour, where he defeated all challengers and was admired by millions of fans. Considered one of the greatest athletic heroes of all time, Gotch soon made wrestling the nation's most popular sport.

Frank Gotch was one of this century's first pro wrestlers.

Weight, balance, and agility are just as important in wrestling as strength.

Getting Started

You are in the ring. It is the start of a match. Dressed in tight elastic togs and soft shoes, you stand on a padded mat, alone except for your opponent and the referee. You might be wearing light headgear to protect your ears from the constant rubbing resulting from headlocks. Your opponent is your own size. He wants to dump you on your back and pin you as much as you want to pin him. You have practiced your moves endlessly and conditioned your body to perfection, waiting for this moment. The next six minutes will be furious and grueling, as you test yourself one-on-one in the ring.

If this sounds like a sport you would like to try, talk to your gym teacher at school about joining a wrestling program. Most schools have wrestling teams, as do scouting organizations, community centers, and the YMCA. Wrestling is a sport that calls for training and a lot of practice. It is a tough, strenuous sport that requires good coaching. Serious wrestling should not be attempted without supervision.

Having stepped into the ring with your opponent, you meet in the center and shake hands. The referee blows his whistle and signals "wrestle." Your goal— the object of a wrestling match—is to pin your opponent's shoulder blades to the mat. To do this, you will use a number of grips and holds you have worked on so many times that you can do them in your sleep. These maneuvers, known as *takedowns*, involve lifting, tripping, tackling, throwing and twisting your opponent. He, of course, is doing everything he can to counterattack. His goal is to convert your offensive moves to his advantage. Likewise, if he is attacking, then you will counter his moves, seeking a defensive advantage. Strength is important in wrestling, but quickness and a knowledge of leverage are more important. Leverage is knowing—and making the most of—your opponent's weaknesses.

Rules of the Game

The first period begins with both wrestlers standing. The second period begins from the *referee's position*. In the referee's position, one wrestler is down on his hands and knees in the center of the ring. The referee tosses a coin to see who will be up or down. The up wrestler, also on his knees, takes a position by his left side. He wraps his right arm around his opponent's torso and, with his left hand, grips the back of his opponent's left arm, as if he were about to pop his elbow. The position is reversed at the start of the third period.

The wrestler who gets the first takedown wins two points. Each contestant gets two points for his first takedown, and one point for each additional takedown. It is the bottom or down wrestler's aim to escape or reverse his position. An *escape* is worth one point. A *reversal* is worth two, because he breaks free of the up wrestler's hold, and comes out on top, as well. Their positions are switched.

A pin occurs if one wrestler's shoulder blades are held to the mat for two seconds. The referee slaps his hand to the mat, and the match is over. The one who is pinned loses. It is not a pin if the shoulders roll from one to the other. If a pin does not occur, the match continues through three two-minute periods—with short rest breaks in between. If no one achieves a pin in that time, the match is awarded—just like a boxing match—on points.

A wrestler in the down position tries to stand-up, while his opponent in the up position tries to pin him.

A wrestler can avoid a touch fall by keeping one or both shoulders at least four inches off the mat.

The contortions that wrestlers get into are sometimes comical, but the contestants aren't laughing.

Wrestlers also win three points for a *near fall*, and two points for a *predicament*. A near fall occurs when the top wrestler holds one shoulder to the mat, and the other shoulder is held to within one inch or less of the mat. A predicament is when the top wrestler has control of his opponent in a pin position: either both shoulders are within four inches of the mat, or one shoulder touches and the other is within 45 degrees. Additionally, one point is given to the top man if he maintains advantage for more than one minute.

Points can also be awarded to your opponent if you use illegal holds or engage in unnecessary roughness or unsportsmanlike conduct. In no-pin matches won on points, draws are quite common.

There are times, in the course of a match, when the down wrestler—sensing danger—will try to move outside the circle. At other times, in the heat of the action, both wrestlers will move out of the circle. If the referee judges that the down man moved out on purpose, that wrestler loses a point for *stalling*. The match resumes in the center of the ring, with the wrestlers taking up the referee's position, according to their down-up positions when the action was stopped. If, in a furious struggle, both wrestlers move out of the circle, and the referee does not call a stalling foul, the wrestlers resume the down-up positions they held at the beginning of the period.

Diet and Nutrition

The wrestler's first rule of conditioning is to eat good, healthy food. Diet and nutrition are important for strength, energy, and stamina. Wrestlers also need to be constant weight watchers. Because they compete in specific weight brackets, wrestlers sometimes move up or down to different levels. In high school competition, for example, the brackets range in 10-pound intervals from a low of 75 pounds and under to a high of 200 pounds and more. At the college level, the range runs in 10-pound intervals from 120 pounds to 190 pounds.

Big wrestlers who carry a lot of body weight often have trouble maintaining their meet weight. Their goal is to weigh as little as possible without sacrificing strength and energy. Smaller wrestlers who want to compete in a heavier weight bracket will try to put on a few pounds without giving up their quickness and agility.

A young wrestler should always talk to his coach about a weight control program first. So-called "crash" diets to lose weight or "pigging out" to gain weight are not the way to develop a sound, healthy body. A balanced diet should be maintained at all times. This is especially true for a young wrestler who is still growing. He should be working to build up his body, not breaking it down. Because the nutritional needs of individual body types are different, each wrestler should devise a personal daily diet plan that has the proper combination of calories, proteins, minerals, and vitamins. Many dietary supplements for gaining weight, and appetite suppressants for losing weight, are not healthy approaches to weight control. Steroids for building up muscle are dangerous drugs that should never be taken. Remember, never make a drastic change in your eating habits without first talking to a doctor to find out what your body needs for good health.

Conditioning

Wrestling demands more of an athlete physically than any other sport. Football coaches often recommend that their players take up wrestling as a way to get in shape! Conditioning programs include a mix of calisthenics, weight lifting, and gymnastic exercises. The training schedule is designed to improve a wrestler's strength, agility, flexibility, power, balance, and endurance.

For wrestlers younger than high school age, weight training is generally not

Good nutrition and conditioning are important to a wrestler's success.

recommended. Most coaches advise young people to hold off on lifting weights until they have reached puberty. Their muscles and bone structures are still developing, and pumping iron can do more damage than good.

A wrestler's daily training and practice session falls into three parts: warm-up, weight lifting, and drills in individual wrestling skills. The warm-up period is used to increase blood circulation and stretch the muscles, which helps prevent injuries. A typical warm-up includes such exercises as jogging, jumping jacks, twisting from side to side, toe touching, sit-ups, leg lifts, and push-ups.

Pumping iron is usually limited to two or three days per week. After this kind of strenuous activity, the muscles need a day to rest. Because wrestling demands that an athlete be in top condition from his toes to his head, all the major muscle groups are given a workout. These muscle groups are the arms, chest, back, abdominals, and legs. Wrestlers also spend a lot of time building up their neck muscles.

Wrestling is a sport of endurance. This contestant looks beaten, but he eventually won this match.

A gymnastic exercise program is often used on the days following weight training. These are rigorous activities including rope-climbing (hands only) to a height of 20 feet, and chin-ups with extra weight—such as a dumbbell or medicine ball—added to the wrestler's body. Other exercises include handstand presses, which are like push-ups from a handstand position; and dips, which are like push-ups performed in an upright position on the parallel bars.

These are but a few of the exercises used in a complete conditioning program. All coaches use different programs that they have designed after years of experience in trying to bring out the best in their wrestlers. Although the pin is the quickest and surest way to victory on the mat, most wrestling contests are won or lost in the final period, with physical conditioning being the deciding factor. A wrestler cannot be content with just being able to hang in there—to wrestle for six minutes. He must be able to go all-out in the third period, to pour it on—even to come from behind, if he is down on points.

The Coach

Many a great athlete will tell you that they wouldn't have achieved their successes without a great coach. One coach that surely belongs in that category is former Olympic and All-American wrestling coach Roy Pittman. Now based in Portland, Oregon, Pittman runs a wrestling program that is the model for more than 100 other registered wrestling clubs in that state. Open to everyone, Pittman's Peninsula Park wrestling program has young students from all over Oregon. All of them want to be a "Pitt Man." An average of 70 to 80 students show up for his practices in a gym barely big enough for one full-size mat. No one is turned away.

Like many wrestling coaches, Pittman is a philosopher. It is a philosophy about winning and success that has nothing to do with what happens in the ring. "If our purpose is to make this world a better place, then athletics should teach you not only how to compete, but also who you are competing against—which is yourself, and your last performance. For that is the true victory. I couldn't care less about winning matches."

In fact, outside of practice and away from the wrestling mat, Pittman talks mostly about wrestling as a way to self-improvement. He founded his program on the idea of "redefining winning."

The importance of an inspirational coach before, during, and after a grueling match cannot be underestimated.

"Winning is not getting your hand raised," he explains. "Winning is doing the best you can with what you have at a given time. I have a philosophy that, during the first year, you learn how to lose; the next, how to win; the next year, how to be a gentleman."

For Pittman, wrestling and life are inseparable. "Physically, I started wrestling when I was 14," he says, adding, "but I really began at birth, wrestling to take that next breath. Also, I wrestled to not buy into the prejudices that people have."

When asked what the sport has meant to him, he replies: "Wrestling has helped keep me focused and balanced. In tough situations, we all wrestle to make the right choice. I am not afraid to wrestle to make the right choice...Also, [wrestling] has taught me how to give, and to be more sensitive to the needs of other people."

After college, where he played baseball, Pittman returned to his community to make a contribution. He wanted to work with inner city youth. He needed a sport that could help him teach his values, but one that did not cost a lot of money. "Wrestling is a sport that everyone can do, where everyone can have success," he says. "All the other sports—football, basketball, baseball—you have to have certain skills. Wrestling is the only sport where discipline and dedication is stronger than athleticism."

All of Pittman's practice sessions end with what he calls a "mental session." It is here that his real work begins. "We define family," he says. "We define goals. We empower kids to empower themselves. The biggest thing is, we teach kids how to accept success, because success comes in many forms. Wrestling teaches us how to accept ourselves, and also how to take our strengths and build upon them. Most people do not know what their strengths are. Wrestling helps to discover and define those individual strengths."

When asked what a young wrestler can do on his own when he is not in the gym, Pittman replies: "Get in tune with yourself. Life is all about attitude. Practice loving and caring. Practice looking at things differently. We are an excuse-oriented society, and with wrestling there are no excuses. You have to learn to take responsibility for the choices you make—period. Above all, learn to love yourself. Love yourself enough to do the right thing."

A successful takedown is easy to describe but more difficult to achieve in a real match.

Maneuvers and Drills

CHAPTER THREE

Once a wrestler is in top physical shape, he must master a variety of mat skills in order to succeed. His security in these two aspects of the sport will give him confidence, courage, determination, and heart. The only way to achieve this goal is through hard work and dedication. A good wrestler approaches his practice and study of technique like a scientist.

Wrestling skills can be broken down into three basic categories: takedowns, escapes and reversals, and pins. Most coaches have a personal philosophy about the right way to approach these skills, and the way they should be performed. One coach, for example, might take an offensive philosophy, putting a lot of emphasis on takedowns. He believes that matches are won or lost on the most fundamental move. Another coach might believe that the ability to escape and reverse position—a defensive move—is more important.

Staying on the offensive is a common coaching philosophy.

But whatever a coach's perspective, a thorough knowledge of a limited number of carefully selected skills is essential to good wrestling. A personal system or strategy must be built on a solid understanding and execution of basic moves.

These maneuvers are learned day in, day out in practice, as team members wrestle each other in drills. Each maneuver is made up of a series of specific movements. It is important to remember that the maneuver will only be as good as the weakest position or movement in the series—in the way that a chain is only as strong as its weakest link.

The Takedown

A wrestling match begins with both wrestlers in a standing position, maneuvering for a takedown. Because the wrestler who wins the takedown will have the initial advantage, many coaches believe the takedown to be all-important. Experience has shown that winning wrestlers are the ones who get the takedown and keep offensive pressure on their opponents. The takedown artist is an aggressive wrestler who is always on the attack.

In the course of a match, the takedown is considered the most difficult phase. The first thing a wrestler has to do is perfect his stance. Although his main objective is to attack, he must be prepared to counter his opponent's aggression as well. Whatever stance he chooses, he must be able to maneuver in comfort. Once a wrestler finds a stance that suits him, he must stick with it and begin working on technique.

FIVE BASIC STANCES

1) The square stance: The feet are shoulder width and even, knees slightly bent, leaning forward at the waist, with arms out and palms up.

2) Open stance number 1: Feet shoulder width with the left foot slightly forward, knees bent, back straight, with arms out and palms down.

3) Open stance number 2: Feet shoulder width apart with the left foot forward—like a right-handed hitter in the batter's box—knees bent, back straight, with arms out and palms out flat, facing the opponent.

4) The knee stance: Down on one knee—like a football lineman—the other leg up, body leaning forward with the left arm for support.

5) The closed stance: When the wrestlers have come together, gripping neck and elbow.

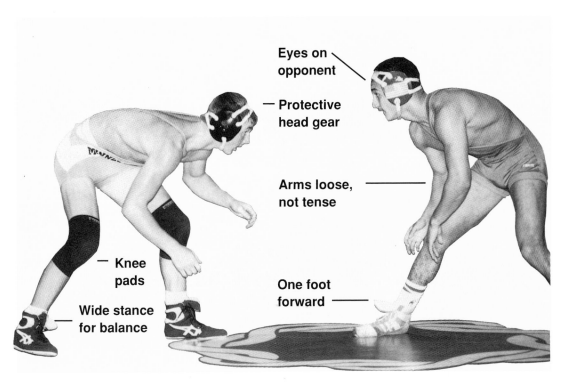

Eyes on opponent

Protective head gear

Arms loose, not tense

Knee pads

One foot forward

Wide stance for balance

The open stance is one of the most common positions to assume at the start of a match.

John Smith of the USA Olympic team assumes the knee stance during a Barcelona match.

Wrestlers try to tie-up their opponent with a variety of grips and holds.

In each of these stances, certain rules must be followed: The head is always up, with eyes on the opponent's middle. The weight is distributed evenly on the balls of the feet, maintaining good foot control so the wrestler can move and circle his opponent. He keeps his movement free of any pattern. The hands are out front and moving, and the wrestler—elbows in—tries to remain within arm's distance of his opponent.

Seeking a takedown, a wrestler has several choices of attack strategy. He may go for his opponent's arms and shoulders, his head, or his legs. The art of the takedown lies in timing. A wrestler must know when to "shoot in" on his opponent. If he chooses the wrong moment, he might wind up on his back.

There are intermediate steps to the takedown. The first is called the *tie-up*, and the second is called the *set-up*. In the tie-up, the wrestlers make initial contact and grip each other in certain ways, looking for an advantage that will lead to the takedown. Some tie-up positions are the "monkey on a stick tie-up," "inside double arm tie-up," and "head shrug tie-up." The initial movement of the tie-up begins with the wrestler walking toward his opponent, making loose contact with his hands, and moving his arm up to the back of the opponent's neck. In a sense, the wrestlers are getting a feel for one another, getting ready to make their moves.

If a wrestler does not feel comfortable with his tie-up, he backs out and starts over, looking for a set-up. In a set-up, a wrestler tries to put his opponent off balance. He may do this with a fake. If the opponent reacts to the fake, he will be caught off guard and open to a swift offensive takedown move. The goal of mastering the set-up is to try one maneuver, with the intention of making it good, but having the knowledge and control to use it as a fake or a set-up for a second move, if the first is countered. This principle is true of all wrestling. Wrestling requires moves built upon other moves. A good wrestler can use a variety of moves in various combinations.

Wrestlers strive to force their opponent off balance. A good wrestler always tries to keep his head up.

There are dozens of variations on these attacks, as well as many moves to counter them. Some arm-and-shoulder attack maneuvers have names such as "lateral drop," "elbow throw," "whizzer hip lock," and "double hook throw." Takedown maneuvers for attacking the head are called "head throw," "duck under," and "head shuck." When going for an opponent's legs, a few of the maneuvers used are the "double leg pickup," "single leg pickup," and the "fireman's carry."

Regardless of the attack approach used, a good wrestler will always keep certain principles in mind when attempting a takedown. He will always make the first move, but he will not do so by reaching for his opponent, which could lead to his own downfall. He will not push his opponent, which could give his opponent the advantage of momentum. He will always put his hands on top of an opponent's head, neck, or back. His hands will be brought down on an opponent, like a bear, rather than up, as a bull might do, hooking with its horns. He will keep his head higher than that of his opponent, and keep him face to face. Moving constantly, he will avoid moving in predictable ways.

Counters, or defensive moves against a takedown, are usually learned after a wrestler has mastered the takedown. This ensures that a wrestler will maintain his aggressiveness, and not slide into defensive strategy. Some counter moves include the "leg back," "whip over," and "quarter nelson."

Because the takedown is so important, some coaches stress takedown drills in their practices. They might have a team takedown tournament, when all wrestling is done in the standing or neutral position, for one-minute periods. As soon as a takedown is gained, the match is stopped and the wrestlers start over. The winner is the first to gain two out of three takedowns. In other drills, one wrestler might have his eyes closed, or his hands behind his back, to develop his countering skills.

Escapes and Reversals

Takedowns are offensive moves. *Escapes* and *reversals* are defensive attempts to get out of a successful takedown or any other threatening down position. Balance is fundamental to the underneath position. In the takedown, it is important to know when to attack. In the escape, it is important to know when to move out.

One type of escape—the sit out—is shown here.

A wrestler nearly on his stomach is in danger of losing the match. Notice how the down man is trying to keep his shoulders off the mat.

The worst positions for the down man, listed in order of least mobility and greatest danger, are:

1) on the back;
2) on the stomach;
3) on the side;
4) on the buttocks; and
5) on one or both knees.

These positions are to be avoided at all costs. The safest position for any wrestler is on his feet, which is as far away from a pin as one can get. Thus, many coaches teach their wrestlers to move upward when trapped in a down position.

The five down positions can serve as a guide to selecting the proper escape move. Once a wrestler has been maneuvered into a down position, he can resort to certain techniques to help himself. Even though he is at a disadvantage, the down man should continue to work to keep his opponent on the defensive. For example, his hands and legs should always be kept free. He should try to keep his head up and his hips low. He should never lie flat on his stomach or on his side. Sitting positions are also to be avoided.

Many escape maneuvers begin from the referee's position, where one opponent automatically begins in the down position. The bottom man must break the hold and attempt to stand up, thereby returning to a neutral position. One of the most common escape techniques for this position is the "sit out."

On his hands and knees, with his opponent's arm around his torso, the down man quickly slides his inside leg out front, directly in line with the top wrestler. Rolling on his hip and elbow, he brings his trailing knee over and plants his foot, turns to face his opponent, and stands up. When his leg is out he looks like a ballplayer sliding into base. Keep in mind that the top man is doing everything he can to make sure the down man does not escape. To every move there is a countermove, which is why all moves must be executed perfectly.

Other escape maneuvers from the referee's position are the "side roll," "short switch," and "stand-up." If the down wrestler escapes, leaving the wrestlers in a neutral position, he wins a point. If in his escape he also manages to become the top man, he has a reversal, and receives two points. Practice drills consist of two wrestlers taking the referee's position, then working each escape maneuver through its various countermoves.

Breakdowns, Rides, and the Pin

The pin is the surest way to victory on the mat. It is not, however, every wrestler's ultimate goal. Because most matches are won on points, the pin can be of secondary importance to takedowns, escapes, and reversals. A wrestler who can take his man down and escape from him has the best chance of winning—with or without a pin. The strategy is to outclass the opponent and wear him down, building up points along the way.

The up man uses his weight to ride his opponent until he can force him down for a fall or near fall.

In some wrestling programs for youngsters, coaches begin lessons with the pin, rather than the takedown. This strategy gives the young wrestler close-in mat experience and pin technique. It also helps prevent injuries. Beginners who do not know how to fall properly can get hurt in takedown exercises.

Because all major wrestling moves are a sequence of small moves, the pin begins at the beginning, with the referee's position. The top man's objective is to keep his weight on his opponent and gain a *breakdown*. In a sense, he is trying to "unlock" the down man's defensive position. He wants to break him down—to get him stretched out flat on the mat—so that he can effect a pin. The down man can be thought of as a table, with the four table legs being his hands and knees. Just as a table cannot stand on two legs, the top man tries to disable a leg and an arm of his opponent, thereby forcing him to the mat.

Head-to-head in a match, as the top man struggles for a breakdown, the down man tries to escape. For every breakdown maneuver there is a countermove. Once the breakdown is achieved, the top man presses into his opponent with his chest, legs wide for good balance and support, and drives him down further. He can then begin to maneuver his opponent into pin position. This is called a *ride*. The top man keeps his weight on the down man, riding him, seeking a final hold that will enable him to make the pin. At this stage in the match, the action can slow down when the down man cannot escape, and the top man cannot make the pin.

There are many breakdown-and-ride techniques. They have names such as "grapevine," "chicken wing," and "head lever." Most of them call for a variety of ankle, knee, leg, and arm grips on the part of the top man. Breakdowns and rides lead into pinning combinations such as the "cradle" and the "half nelson." It is not easy to hold an opponent down to the mat, so pin holds can be quite complex, with the wrestlers looking like pretzels.

Try to imagine pinning an opponent. Suppose that he is lying flat on his back, unresisting. Slip one arm under his neck, and the other under his knees, as if you were going to carry him away. This is the basic cradle position. You are at ninety degrees to his body. Now, join your hands in a wristlock, which will bring your opponent's knees up to his chin. Rising on your toes, lean into the back of his raised legs. He cannot move. There is no escape. He is pinned.

To succeed with a pin, the top man must always keep his weight on his opponent. He must keep his weight low and his knees off the mat, moving with his feet. He must be sure never to anchor himself to his opponent, and to keep moving—constantly changing his pin combination. A good strategy for the top man is to control his opponent's legs. A down man cannot move very far or very fast if his legs are tied up.

he challenge of winning an Olympic gold medal is the dream of every wrestler.

Tournaments and Heroes

CHAPTER FOUR

During the early part of the twentieth century, freestyle wrestling was a professional, "pay for play" sport. Early mat heroes such as Tom Jenkins and Frank Gotch were international celebrities. In 1911, wrestling for the world championship, Gotch defeated a Russian named George Hackenschmidt in a match seen by over 30,000 Chicago fans. After Gotch's death in 1917, however, wrestling went into decline. It became less of a sport and more and more like carnival entertainment provided by modern "professional" wrestlers such as Hulk Hogan.

Today, freestyle wrestling is a strictly amateur sport that remains true to its noble origins and traditions. It is governed around the world by the International Wrestling Federation (FILA) and nationally by USA Wrestling. In the United States, in terms of number of participants, wrestling is the eighth largest high school sport and the fifth largest college sport. For the young wrestler, the sport of wrestling offers championships and tournaments to dream about, as well as heroes to emulate and live up to.

When the modern Olympics began in 1896, wrestling was one of nine sports on the agenda—an indication of its stature as a classic sport. Only two countries, however, entered the event. Fortunately, these early wrestlers were in the same weight class. In recent years, the increasing popularity of wrestling has brought with it three additional major meets: the World Championships, the Pan-American Games, and the World Cup. These are significant contests, but an Olympic gold medal remains every wrestler's highest hope.

Olympic mat men wrestle according to international freestyle rules, which combine the Greco-Roman and freestyle maneuvers. Olympic wrestlers

Watching two "weaponless warriors" compete strenuously for six minutes is one of the most exciting moments in sports.

are allowed to use their legs—unlike Greco-Roman wrestlers—but a touch fall, rather than a pin fall, determines the victor.

Held each year (except for Olympic years) in a different country, the World Championships showcase the finest of both Greco-Roman and freestyle wrestling. Although it is still controversial, most United States wrestling authorities cite 1961 as being the first year of the officially recognized World Championships. An international meet that had been going on for several decades, the United States did not compete until 1961 and did not win a gold medal until 1969.

Buenos Aires, Argentina, was the site of the first Pan-American Games in 1951. Every four years the nations of the Western Hemisphere get together for their own special Olympics. Offering both Greco-Roman and freestyle wrestling, these games are a major event for champion wrestlers from the United States.

The World Cup is an annual freestyle tournament started in 1973 by American coach Joseph Scalzo. Scalzo had a dream of building a tournament by inviting wrestlers from North America, South America, Europe, Asia, and

Africa. Over the years, Scalzo's meet has become one of the most competitive events in wrestling. For most of its history, the World Cup has been held in his hometown of Toledo, Ohio.

American Tournaments

There are at least ten major American wrestling tournaments, most of them governed by university organizations such as the NCAA and NAIA. The NCAA Division I meet is the top goal for college wrestlers.

Outside the college wrestling scene, the United States Freestyle Senior Open and the AAU National Freestyle Championships are open to all amateur wrestlers. The AAU tournament, which began in 1888, is the oldest in the United States. The Senior Open originated in 1969. Some observers consider it the roughest of all wrestling tournaments.

The largest tournament in the world is the Junior Olympic Wrestling Championships (the Junior Nationals) which is the pinnacle of high school mat prowess. Started in 1971 in Iowa City, Iowa, the Junior Nationals annually host upward of 2,000 wrestlers from nearly every state. These young mat men have almost 4,000 matches in five days. More than 1,000 volunteers are needed to keep the matches running smoothly.

Wrestling is one of the most popular sports in college today.

Danny Hodge was one of the most successful wrestlers from the United States during the 1950s.

The Wrestling Hall of Fame

Frank Gotch was so good that he inspired wrestlers to organize the sport according to weight and size. They also began dividing themselves into amateur and professional camps and laying down rules. Choke and submission holds were barred, and time periods were shortened. Amateur wrestling clubs and organizations were formed, and the sport became popular in high schools and colleges. While amateur wrestling thrived, however, professional wrestling became gimmicky and theatrical. True sports fans turned away from the overacted, staged events, and amateur wrestling became the showcase of champions.

In 1976, the National Wrestling Hall of Fame opened in Stillwater, Oklahoma. It honors and celebrates the great wrestlers of this century, and gives young wrestlers heroes to look up to. Young ballplayers have Babe Ruth and Hank Aaron to look up to, while young wrestlers have Dan Gable and Bobby Douglas. Here are but a few of the wrestling legends who are honored in the Hall of Fame.

Danny Hodge

In 1956, the 177-pound Hodge won the NCAA title, the AAU Greco-Roman championship, and the freestyle championship—all in only ten days. He won every match by a fall. That same year at the Melbourne Olympics, he won a silver medal. During his years at the University of Oklahoma Hodge never lost, winning 36 of 46 bouts by a fall. He was a three-time NCAA champion, and was twice voted the tournament's Outstanding Wrestler.

Sports writers speak with awe of Hodge's power, strength, and skill. He completely dominated his opponents. During his career, no one ever took him down from a standing position. His grip was legendary, strong enough to squeeze "water from a stone." As if his wrestling achievements were not enough, after his college days Hodge went on to win AAU and Golden Gloves boxing titles! He is the only athlete ever to have done so.

Terry McCann

McCann is one of those athletes who truly defines amateur greatness. As a champion wrestler, coach, and organizer of the sport, his contributions are many. At the age of 12, he began wrestling in a Chicago community program. Winning one high school title after another, he proceeded to the University of Iowa, where he won two NCAA championships. A lightweight at 115 pounds, McCann later wrestled for the YMCA in Tulsa, Oklahoma, winning three national titles. At the 1960 Rome Olympics, he won it all with a gold medal in the 125.5-pound class.

After coaching high school wrestling for several years, McCann went home to Chicago where he supervised the Mayor Daley Youth Foundation Club. In seven years his teams won six national freestyle and five Greco-Roman meets. In 1965 he was one of the founding fathers of the United States Wrestling Federation, the governing body of today's amateur wrestling.

Russell Vis

Vis is one of Terry McCann's boyhood inspirations. A high school champion, Vis had no college experience. Wrestling as an amateur up and down the West Coast, he won every club, city, and regional meet he entered. He paid his own way from tournament to tournament. An unknown, Vis traveled to the East Coast in 1921, and won the national freestyle tournament. Then he did it again for three more years, never losing a bout. In 1924 he capped his reign with an Olympic gold medal, wrestling in the 145-pound class. A self-made wrestler, Vis spent his later years promoting youth wrestling.

Harold Nichols

One of the great coaches of all time, Nichols is famous for his career at Iowa State University. Once a collegiate champion himself, in 1953 Nichols started his own coaching program at ISU and built it into a dynasty for the next two decades.

During Nichols' reign, his teams won nearly 400 dual meet victories. From 1969 through 1973, the Iowa Cyclones won four out of five national trophies. Nichols' career also includes seven runner-up national championship teams, and seven of his wrestlers went on to Olympic heroics—winning two gold medals, one silver, and one bronze.

Nichols received the Coach of the Year award four times, but he is best remembered for his untiring promotion of wrestling as a healthy sport. Nichols worked with the AAU and the U.S. Olympic Committee to help bring championship wrestling into the modern era.

Robin Reed

Like all sports fans, wrestling fans argue endlessly about who was the best. Reed's name is never overlooked. A contemporary of Vis (but a few pounds lighter), Reed's mat prowess is legendary. A 125-pound high school champion, he wrestled for Oregon State University, where he dominated national tournaments from 1921 to 1924. Like Vis, he captured a gold medal in the 1924 Paris Olympics, winning every Olympic match by a pin. In fact, during his Olympic training Reed pinned nearly every member of his team! He even pinned the 191-pounder and the heavyweight—both of whom were also gold medalists!

Rick Sanders

Sanders heads the list of all-time wrestling favorites. An unbeatable lightweight and oddball personality, he is remembered for his actions off the mat as well as on. Through the 1960s, there was no other wrestler like him. As a three-time Oregon high school champion, he won 80 matches and lost only one. At Portland State University, he won the NAIA championship in 1965, Division II NCAA titles in 1967 and 1968, and Division I titles in 1966 and 1967. As a first year college student, he won a national freestyle title and made the U.S. World team.

These achievements would seem to be enough for any wrestler, but for Sanders they were just a beginning. He won four more national titles and six medals in international meets, including a Pan-American Games title and a silver medal at the 1968 Olympics. In 1969 he was the first American to ever win a gold medal at the World Championships.

Off the mat, Sanders was known as a free thinker. He had long hair, a beard, and a training style that made his coaches shudder. On the way to big meets, friends recall him running up and down the aisle of the airplane to get in shape. A generous spirit who was always willing to give his time to helping young wrestlers, Sanders would put on free clinics at the hint of a grappling question.

Perhaps this story will explain the man: In 1970, weighing in at 125.5 pounds, Sanders took the world team trials in a grueling series of bouts with Don Behm. Behm, a world and Olympic medalist himself, was much needed on the U.S. team. In hope of enabling them both to wrestle and strengthen the team, Sanders gave up the 125.5-pound spot and tried to cut to 114.5—unsuccessfully. In 1972, while hitchhiking through Europe after the Munich Olympics, Sanders died tragically in a car accident.

Rick Sanders inspired many young wrestlers in the late 1960s and early '70s.

Dan Gable

Of all the great Hall of Fame wrestlers, Gable stands out as the picture of dedication, desire, and perfection. During his career he won every championship open to an American athlete, and was acclaimed the "World's Greatest Wrestler." If asked about the secret of his success, Gable will reply, "Hard work, hard work, hard work."

Gable grew up in Iowa, where he was a three-time high school wrestling champion. As a student at Iowa State University he won 100 matches in a row! One of the few matches he ever lost was a 6-0 decision to Rick Sanders in the 1967 AAU championships. Beginning in 1969, he won three national freestyle titles, and two years later won gold medals at the World Championships and Pan-American Games. After thousands of miles of roadwork and tens of thousands of hours of rigorous training—three workouts daily year round—the stage was set for his gold medal attempt. At the 1972 Munich Olympics, wrestling in the 149.5-pound class, his dream came true.

Like many champion wrestlers, Gable turned to coaching after his retirement. In 1977 he became the head coach at the University of Iowa, and in 1980 he served as coach of the U.S. Olympic team. "One cannot wrestle effectively with a tired mind or with untrained instincts," Gable writes in the introduction to his biography. "The instincts are developed reflectively, studiously, then drilled for mastery....The lazy minded wrestler is a loser. Let those who are tired defect. They only discredit the art. But those who would make great sacrifices to win, the sport is made for you—follow me."

Bobby Douglas

Douglas is one of those athletes who breaks a barrier with every new challenge. He is the complete wrestler. As his book, *The Making of a Champion*, shows, Douglas knows just about everything regarding wrestling history and technique. In 1964 he became the first African-American to wrestle on the U.S. Olympic team, and in 1992 he became that team's coach.

Douglas was born in a small, eastern Ohio town. As a small boy he watched his grandfather get together with his coal mining pals to wrestle outdoors alongside the railroad tracks. His grandfather noticed the six-year-old's enthusiasm for the sport and started him on a program of rugged drills. He told young Dan wonderful stories about the traditions of African wrestling.

Douglas' grandfather died when the boy was eight, but the love of wrestling never left him. Several years later, his high school coach took him on as a junior wrestler, and coached him into winning two state championships. After a couple of years at West Virginia State College, Douglas transferred to Oklahoma State where he earned a degree in health and physical education.

Named team captain, Douglas placed fourth in the 1964 Tokyo Olympics. After winning a silver medal in the 1966 World Championships, he became a favorite to win the gold in the 1968 Olympics held in Mexico City. Unfortunately, a bad case of food poisoning ruined his Olympic hopes. Named the outstanding wrestler in the United States in 1970, Douglas retired with a record of 303-17-7. In 1973 he became the first African-American to coach a

Olympic coach Bobby Douglas is the most famous African-American wrestler of the twentieth century.

major college wrestling team, at the University of California at Santa Barbara. In 1974 he moved on to Arizona State, where he is currently coaching varsity wrestlers. In his spare time, he coaches the Sunkist Kids, a young people's club that has won the national freestyle championship seven times in eight years.

Today, Douglas is the nation's most powerful advocate of the wrestling culture as a physical, mental, and spiritual way of life. When not speaking about his African ancestors, he talks about people like George Washington, Genghis Khan, Norman Schwarzkopf, and Plato—wrestlers one and all.

Bobby Douglas, Dan Gable, Rick Sanders—with champions like these as examples of success, all a young wrestler needs is confidence in himself, dedication to the sport, and the will to work hard.

Glossary

Amateur Athletics Union (AAU). The oldest governing body for organized amateur sports in the United States.

Breakdown. A wrestling move in which the up man tries to break his opponent's defensive position, seeking further advantage and, ultimately, a pin.

Counters. Defensive moves against a takedown.

Decision. A wrestling victory won by points, rather than by a pin or touch fall.

Down man. The wrestler who is underneath his opponent and at a disadvantage.

Draw. A match in which neither wrestler pins the other, and both have the same number of points.

Escape. A wrestling move in which the down man manages to get out of the up man's hold.

Leverage. Using balance and an opponent's weight to gain the advantage.

Near fall. When one shoulder is pinned and the other is within one inch of the mat.

Pin or **Pin fall.** A victorious move in which one wrestler holds another's shoulder blades to the mat for a measurable amount of time—usually two seconds.

Predicament. When at least one shoulder is near the mat in a pin position.

Referee's position. The position used to begin the second and third periods of a match, in which one wrestler is down on his hands and knees in the center of the ring, and the other is up, with his arms around the down man. The positions are determined by a referee's coin toss. At the beginning of the third period, the positions are reversed.

Reversal. A wrestling maneuver in which the down man, having escaped the up man's hold, gains the top position.

Ride. When the up man presses his weight onto his opponent to achieve a pin.

Set-up. A move in which one wrestler tries to fake the other out, gaining an advantage in balance and position.

Stalling. When one wrestler intentionally moves or falls outside the mat circle in order to keep from being pinned.

Standing position. The neutral, upright position taken by wrestlers at the beginning of a match, or at any time when the wrestlers have separated and are back on their feet, seeking a takedown.

Takedown. A basic wrestling move in which one wrestler tries to throw the other to the mat.

Tie-up. A hold in the standing position, in which both wrestlers grip one another around the neck and arms.

Touch fall. A victorious move, in which one wrestler makes another's shoulder blades touch the mat for an instant.

Up man. The wrestler who is on top.

For Additional Information

For more information about the sport of wrestling contact,

Canadian Amateur Wrestling Association
333 River Road
Vanier, Ontario, K1L 8H9
(613) 748-5686

National College Athletic Association (NCAA)
P.O. Box 1906
Mission, KS 66201
(913) 384-3220

National Wrestling Hall of Fame
405 W. Hall of Fame Avenue
Stillwater, OK 74075
(405) 377-5339

USA Wrestling
Group A Member, U.S. Olympic Committee
6155 Lehman Dr.
Colorado Springs, CO 80918
(719) 598-8181

The following books will give you more to read about the great sport of wrestling.

Amateur Wrestling Rules in Pictures by Michael Brown. New York: Perigee Books, 1989.

The Encyclopedia of Championship Wrestling Drills by Ray F. Carson. New York, NY: A.S. Barnes and Company, 1974.

Principles of Championship Wrestling by Ray F. Carson and Buel R. Patterson. New York, NY: A.S. Barnes and Company, 1972.

Encyclopedia of American Wrestling by Mike Chapman. Champaign, IL: Leisure Press, 1990.

Coach's Illustrated Guide to Championship Wrestling by Frank S. Kapral. Englewood Cliffs, NJ: Prentice-Hall, 1964.

Learning How: Wrestling by Rummy Macias. Mankato, MN: Creative Educational Society, 1965.

Wrestling Techniques: Takedowns by Richard C. Maertz. New York, NY: A.S. Barnes and Company, 1970.

The Legend of Dan Gable: "The" Wrestler by Russ L. Smith. Milwaukee, WI: Medalist Sports, 1974.

Index